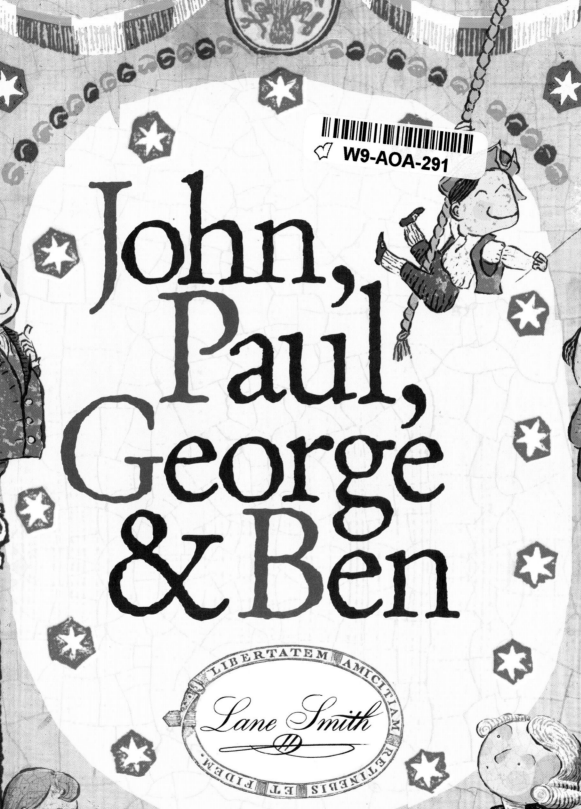

John, Paul, George & Ben

LIBERTATEM AMICITIAM RETINEBIS ET FIDEM

Lane Smith

SCHOLASTIC INC.
New York Toronto London Auckland Sydney Mexico City New Delhi Hong Kong

I get by with a little help from my friends: Special thanks to Alessandra Balzer, Steven Malk, Molly Leach, Mark Egan, Dr. Mary Leach, Anne Diebel, and a big tip of the tricorn hat to Bob Shea. Hear! Hear! Smartest lad in ye olde house.

Once there were four lads:

John, Paul, George, and Ben.*

*Make that *five* lads.

There was also Independent Tom (always off doing his OWN thing).

JOHN

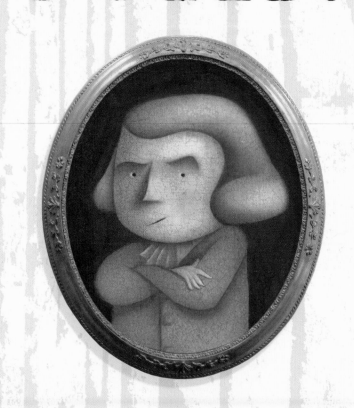

was a *bold* lad.

At the start of every school year the students were asked to write their names on the chalkboard, and every year it was the same story.

"John," his teacher would say, "you have lovely penmanship. John, your confidence is refreshing. But, John, *c'mon . . .*

we don't need to

read it from space!"

PAUL

was a *noisy* lad.

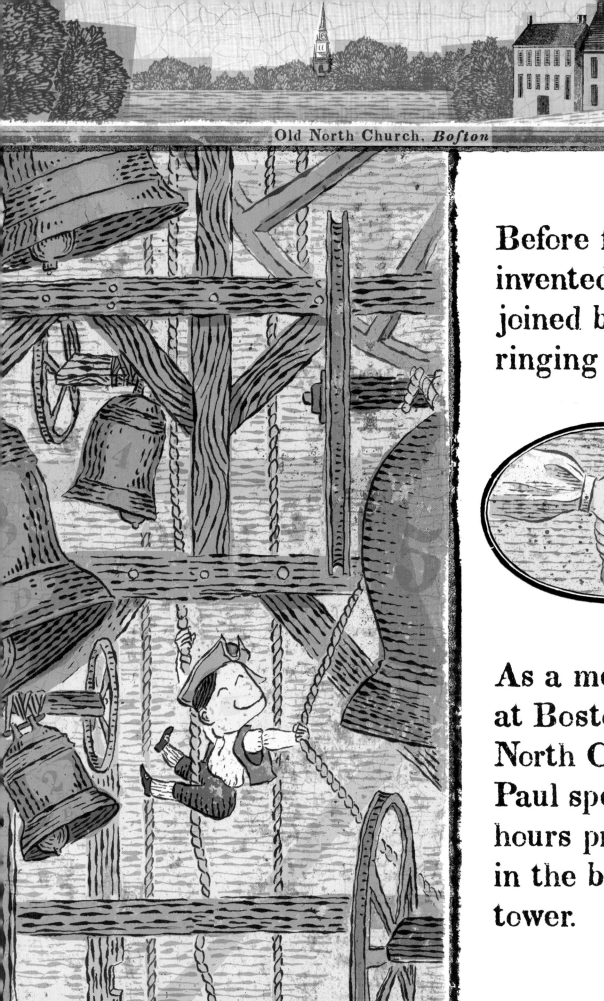

Old North Church, *Boston*

Before fun was invented, people joined bell-ringing clubs.

As a member at Boston's Old North Church, Paul spent hours practicing in the belfry tower.

Over time, that bell-ringing took a toll on young Paul. All day his head was filled with loud *bing*s and *bong*s. He had to practically scream just to hear himself talk.

Now, that's fine around the belfry...

but not at work.

Paul was like a bullhorn in a china shop.

"YOUR **WIG?**
YES, IT'S COMING!

"AND YOUR **POLKA-DOT** SHIRTS ARE COMING! AND THE **PINK** BREECHES ARE COMING!"

THE
RED C
ARE C

people to finally appreciate his special talent.

Everyone except that
big-underwear lady.

She was still mad.

GEORGE

was an *honest* lad.

One day, he took his shiny new hatchet and chopped down his family's cherry tree. When his father discovered the **tree**, he asked, "Son, do you know who killed this **beautiful little cherry tree?**"

"I cannot tell a lie," answered George. "'Twas I who chopped down this **cherry tree.**"

"Then run to my arms, dearest boy," cried his father, "for you have paid me for it a thousand-fold with your **honesty.**"

"Really?" said George.

"**In that case . . .**

when I tell you I've taken out the
made kindling of your carriage,

apple orchard, leveled the barn, and
you'll be a wealthy, wealthy man."

BEN

was a *clever* lad.

Not only did he have a saying for every situation, he generously shared them with anyone. Anywhere. At any time.

He considered it his duty to provide frequent, free advice.

"The sleeping **FOX** catches no poultry!"

"Those who in QUARRELS interpose, must often wipe a bloody nose."

"If your head is WAX don't walk in the SUN."

"THREE can keep a secret if TWO of them are DEAD."

The townsfolk were so taken by his generosity, they came up with a saying especially for Ben...

"PLEASE YOUR BIG

"I like it," said Ben.
"Short and to the point.
Work a **fox** or **turkey**
in there, and **I** think
you've got something."

TOM

was an *independent* lad.

One day his teacher, Mr. Douglas, asked the class to make birdhouses by gluing macaroni to ye olde balsa wood. Tom **HAPPILY** ignored him and used traditional building materials in a neoclassical design.

When the class made a "palm tree," Tom took one look and said, "NOT ON YOUR LIFE!" then quickly left...

to sketch his own tree.

"Young Thomas," fumed teacher Douglas. "Would you mind explaining to the class why you insist on working so independently?" "Certainly," said Tom. "In fact, I've taken the LIBERTY to list the very reasons."

Tom learned the power of his words that day: Mr. Douglas told him to pursue all the LIFE, LIBERTY, and HAPPINESS he wanted . . .

independently in the corner.
The other students pursued lunch.

The rest is **HISTORY**.

Say, you want a revolution? Well, John, Paul, George, Ben, and Tom sure did. In April of 1775, they got one. The Redcoats *were* coming. In fact, King George III's army was marching to Lexington and Concord to arrest John and other *Sons of Liberty....*

Fortunately, Paul Revere was a NOISY man. After his midnight ride, every *Minuteman*, woman, and child knew who was coming and what they'd be wearing. It was the start of the *Revolutionary War*.

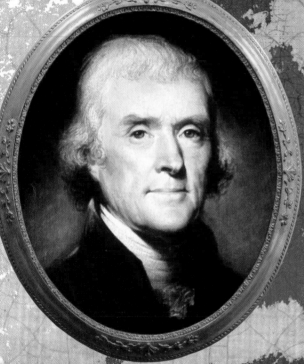

The Americans needed to formally state their separation from the king. Who better than Thomas Jefferson, an INDEPENDENT man, to write the *Declaration of Independence*?

Simply signing such a document was treasonous. And dangerous. Ben Franklin, a CLEVER man, said it best: "*We must all hang together*," he quipped, "*or assuredly we shall all hang separately*."

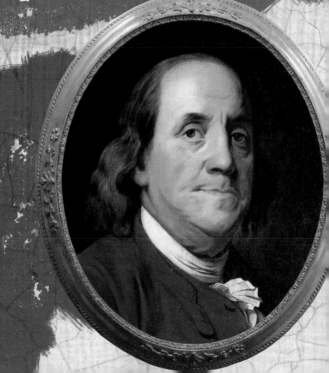

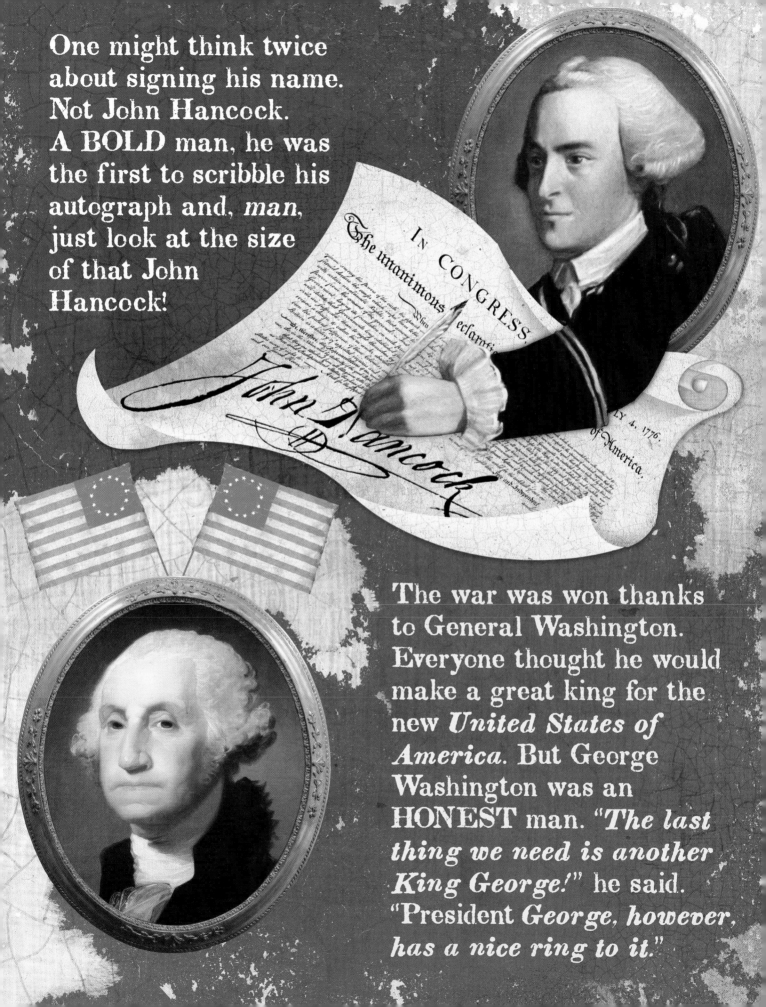

One might think twice about signing his name. Not John Hancock. A BOLD man, he was the first to scribble his autograph and, *man*, just look at the size of that John Hancock!

The war was won thanks to General Washington. Everyone thought he would make a great king for the new *United States of America*. But George Washington was an HONEST man. *"The last thing we need is another King George!"* he said. *"President George, however, has a nice ring to it."*

YE OLDE EPILOGUE

George didn't live in the White House
like all the other presidents.
He was asked to live in New York City...
where there aren't so many trees.

TAKING LIBERTIES

John had the biggest signature on the Declaration of Independence.

[TRUE] *It was so big, he reportedly bragged that the king could read it without his glasses.*

When John was a boy, his signature was always the biggest one on the chalkboard.

[FALSE] *Large, classroom chalkboards weren't invented until a few years later.*

The *Sons of Liberty* was a secret society.

[TRUE] *The patriotic club was formed after King George III imposed the Stamp Tax on the American colonists in 1765. John Hancock was one of the leaders.*

Paul was in a bell-ringing club at the Old North Church.

[TRUE] *We're not sure if this caused him to talk loud, but you try ringing bells nonstop for hours and see how you talk.*

The famous two-if-by-sea lanterns were lit in that same Old North Church, years later, prompting Paul's midnight ride.

[TRUE]

On that night of April 18, 1775, Paul shouted, "The British are coming!"

[FALSE] *Back then, Americans considered themselves British. That would be like saying, "We are coming!" and that sounds pretty silly. Most historians agree he probably said, "The Redcoats are coming!"*

The Revere shop sold extra-large underwear.

[FALSE] *The Revere shop sold silver. But extra-large underwear is always funnier.*

Silver buckles on shoes sure look goofy.

[TRUE]

George chopped down his father's cherry tree.

[FALSE] *This fable was invented by Mason "Parson" Weems (1759–1825). Pretty funny, considering he made up ye olde tale to teach kids a lesson in honesty.*

The phrase "ye olde" gets awfully old after a while.

[TRUE]

When he grew up, George had wooden teeth.

[FALSE] *His fake teeth were made of lots of things like: hippopotamus teeth, gold, lead, and other human teeth.*

George was the only president to serve his full term in New York, not in the White House.

[TRUE]

George was the only president to serve in New York, not in the White House, because New York has fewer trees for him to level.

[FALSE] *We cannot tell a lie: the real reason was because the White House wasn't completed until the second president's term.*

All of Ben's sayings in this book were actual Ben sayings.

[TRUE] *They are all from his Poor Richard's Almanack (1733–1758).*

Besides inventing clever sayings, Ben also invented bifocals, the Franklin stove, the lightning rod, and PlayStation 76.

[TRUE] *Except for that PlayStation part.*

"Work a turkey in there, and I think you've got something!" Instead of an eagle, Ben thought America's national symbol should be a turkey.

[TRUE]

Dullard is a funny word.

[TRUE]

Tom's teacher was named Mr. Douglas.

[TRUE]

Tom's hobbies were architecture and botany.

[TRUE] *The house he eventually designed for himself, Monticello, is a Roman neoclassical masterpiece. Surrounding it are spectacular fruit, flower, and vegetable gardens.*

Every kid should enjoy life, liberty, and the pursuit of happiness.

[TRUE] *As long as your teacher says it's okay.*

The illustrations in this book were hand drawn with pen-and-ink. The textures were created by a variety of techniques, among them, oil paint on canvas and sampled surfaces from handmade parchment papers and weathered pulp boards. The collage elements are facsimiles of eighteenth–century ephemera. All were then combined on a twenty-first–century Macintosh computer.

The miniature portraits of young John, Paul, George, Ben, and Tom were rendered in oil and modeled after their grown-up portraits by Copley, Stuart, and Wright.

The Early American typefaces are from "The Minuteman Printshop" by Walden Font, Winchester, Massachusetts.

YE OLDE PHOTO PERMISSIONS:
John Hancock photograph © Bettman/Corbis

George Washington photograph © Museum of City of New York/Corbis

Thomas Jefferson photograph © Bettman/Corbis

Benjamin Franklin © The Corcoran Gallery of Art/Corbis (Joseph Wright; *Benjamin Franklin*; 1782; oil on canvas; 31 x 25 inches; Corcoran Gallery of Art; Washington, DC; Museum Purchase; Gallery Fund)

Paul Revere photograph © 2006 Museum of Fine Arts, Boston (John Singleton Copley, American, 1738–1815; *Paul Revere* (detail), 1768; Oil on canvas; 89.22 x 72.39 cm [or 35 1/8 x 28 1/2 in]; Museum of Fine Arts, Boston; Gift of Joseph W. Revere, William B. Revere and Edward H.R. Revere, 30.781)

Thanks to these additional illustrations sources: *The American Revolution: A Picture Sourcebook*, by John Grafton (Dover Publications, New York); *Decorative Maps*, by Roderick Barron (Crescent Books, New York).

ISBN: 978-0-545-22167-2

Text and illustrations copyright © 2006 by Lane Smith. All rights reserved. Published by Scholastic Inc., 557 Broadway, New York, NY 10012, by arrangement with Hyperion Books for Children, an imprint of Disney Book Group, LLC. SCHOLASTIC and associated logos are trademarks and/or registered trademarks of Scholastic Inc.

12 11 10 9 8 7 6 5 4 3 2 1   9 10 11 12 13 14/0

Printed in the U.S.A.   40

First Scholastic printing, October 2009

* "I cannot live without books."
—Thomas Jefferson, principal founder of the Library of Congress

"If you would not be forgotten
As soon as you are dead and rotten,
Either write things worth reading,
Or do things worth the writing."
—Benjamin Franklin, founder of America's first lending library

 DESIGNED BY MOLLY LEACH ★